# ISTHMUS TO ABYA YALA

## BOOKS BY ROBERTO HARRISON

*Tropical Lung: exi(s)t(s)* (Omnidawn, 2021)
*Tropical Lung: Mitologia Panameña* (Nion Editions, 2020)
*Yaviza* (Atelos, 2017)
*Bridge of the World* (Litmus Press, 2017)
*culebra* (Green Lantern Press, 2016)
*bicycle* (Noemi Press, 2015)
*Counter Daemons* (Litmus Press, 2006)
*Os* (subpress, 2006)

CITY LIGHTS SPOTLIGHT SERIES NO. 23

# ROBERTO HARRISON

ISTHMUS TO

ABYA YALA

CITY LIGHTS

SAN FRANCISCO

CITY LIGHTS SPOTLIGHT
The City Lights Spotlight Series was founded in 2009,
and is edited by Garrett Caples.

ISBN 978-0-87286-911-0
Library of Congress Control Number: 2023950017

Cover art: Roberto Harrison, *After Reason* [detail] (2023)
Copyright © 2023 by Roberto Harrison

City Lights Books are published at the City Lights Bookstore,
261 Columbus Avenue, San Francisco, CA 94133
www.citylights.com

FOR BRENDA

THERE AND HERE

# CONTENTS

# PREFACE

Summary notes on *Isthmus to Abya Yala*

I AM A MIXED-RACE POET FROM PANAMÁ. MY RACIAL MIXTURE—
red, black, and white—is very common there. I was born in Oregon
to Panamanian parents while my father attended Oregon State Uni-
versity. My family returned to Panamá shortly after I was born. I am
the only person in my immediate family to be born in the United
States. My parents and my sisters were born in Panamá. I was raised
in Panamá until I was seven, at which point we moved to the States, to
Wilmington, Delaware. Spanish was my first language.

The Guna people of Panamá are known for their Molas, which are
a kind of fabric art. Although I do not claim ancestry from the Guna,
Molas are the single most influential art form of my life. The Guna
use the term "Abya Yala" to refer to the Americas (and the Philippines,
Guam, etc.) as it was before the arrival of the Europeans. "Abya Yala"
means something along the lines of "Land in full maturity," "Land of
Life," "Land in Bloom," and also perhaps "Land of Blood," "Land of
Vital Blood," and/or "Land of Life and Abundance." I first learned of
the term Abya Yala through Arysteides Turpana, a friend and Guna
Panamanian poet who died of Covid in 2020. But it wasn't until I
encountered Darrel Alejandro Holnes, a Chocó and Black Panama-
nian American poet, that I began to learn that Abya Yala is already
an international decolonization movement in support of Native and

Black rights. I here propose adding women, LGBTQIA+ people, the disabled, and all oppressed people to the concerns of the movement. First and foremost, for me, at this point, is that Abya Yala is a potent and endlessly generative mystery. Is it already here underlying everything?

In my books I explore what it might mean to be from Panamá in various unconventional ways, with Panamá as snake, as the center link of the bicycle of the hemispheres, as Bridge of the World, as the in-between, as the mind of the earth and as the mind of oceans, as the liminal, as the qubit and the quantum, as the end point of empire, as a link for the Oceans through the Sea . . .

I am currently writing and drawing my *Tropical Lung* septet of books, of which this book is the third to be published. Of the many cultural items belonging to Panamá which I reflect upon in my work, Saloma Panameña (https://youtu.be/fzCdy9Pf0nE) is one of the most valued by my poetics. It provides a sense of reflection and interfacial encounter that I see as the perfect antidote to our current screen mediated lives. For me, Saloma has become an internal way of making from Abya Yala, which includes the many selves and faces inside. To go further, I state that a new kind of Yoga is needed to allow the advanced cyborg to succeed in being human. And a new kind of Yoga is needed to learn to be Abya Yalanses (natives of Abya Yala). "Yoga" here is meant as a putting together, as a putting together of the light and of the dark, and as a putting together of all disparity toward a higher unity. My most fundamental aim is to make dream alliances. And partly I make placeholders for ancient consciousness from Abya Yala to be recovered in the future.

I am making something Mobilian through sevens in *Tropical Lung*. The term "Mobilian" comes from Mabila, which was a Trojan Horse town that proto-Choctaw Tuscaloosa used to lure de Soto into an ambush. Mabila is a new psychic origin for a multiverse as well as the site of one of the first major conflicts between Europeans and Native Americans in North America. In my work, Mabila is also another psychic origin for *Mestizaje* and beyond. A *Mestizaje* for fours (four is a sacred number for many in North America and often implies, among other things, the four colors of mankind, against white supremacy and against the supremacy of any particular color or of any particular mixture, etc.) and for the gourd (the gourd is similarly important to some in Panamá as the circle is here), partly looking toward Louis Riel and the Metís of Canada in how they position themselves in relation to Native traditions—as ally and as respectful honoring relative. A for-all-color *Mestizaje* allied to Abya Yala in dreams and in life. Endless disorder of origin in all directions. Mabila makes mobile an origin state.

Mobilian is a language that is being both found again and created for the first time in making Tecs (my drawings that reflect on face and interface). I am a Tec when I see past the screen. When I find silence then I am a Tec, a citizen of the Tecumseh Republic. There is a Bahá'í temple on a tall thin hill in Panamá just outside of Ciudad de Panamá. It is beautiful in its view. I am not proposing anything in particular in regard to the Bahá'í faith by valuing this temple except that I believe in the higher unity of all spiritual paths. But I see the top of this hill, and especially this temple decorated with Native patterns, as symbolic of the height of the spiritual in Panamá, and as the only entry and the only exit to and from the Tecumseh Republic. Mobilian is an origin language for psychic and symbolic *Mestizaje* moving against racism and toward a more all-inclusive idea of the human, towards the post-human as conceived through the centrality of the animal and of the earth ... *Mestizaje*'s basic reality of mixture extends toward new forms of humanity in Mobilian, whether these forms of humanity be hybrid or not. Mobilian is verb-based and fluid. It is a sound language grown from the earth in Abya Yala. And it is never written and never heard. It grows from an abyss to raise consciousness of interrelation and hidden eternal fires. It is an ur-language of the original face that belongs to the earth here, to Abya Yala now. Mobilian expands considerations of death, with death as more than nothing, with it also as a placeholder for counting and birth inside the ancient worlds of the Americas. Inside of Abya Yala for the future too. This book is a final step in becoming Posthuman Native.

Mobilian takes its root from Mobilian Jargon, a Southeastern North American Muscogean-based trade pidgin language that included words from many Indian languages and eventually included words from European and African languages. The last known fluent speaker of Mobilian Jargon survived until the late twentieth century, which is astonishing to consider as it implies a profound vitality to the languages and to the cultures that it was a part of. Mobilian is internal to Mobilian Jargon. Mobilian is a language in internal life now as it was before. It is the language Tecs use to speak to each other and to work out the cultures and the possibilities of the Tecumseh Republic. By definition, Tecs spawn cultures in Mobilian by organizing around the main principle of generosity, not around greed. William Carlos Williams is the only other poet I know of to consider Mabila (*In the American Grain*). But I was not following William Carlos Williams when I began to consider the imaginal implications of Mabila. I was following my selves.

Some say Mabila was located in what is now southern Alabama. By locating a psychic and symbolic origin at Mabila, I assert that love is always present, even in conflict, even if supremely disguised. In my story, Tuscaloosa won. And so did Tecumseh. (As I show further on in my work, Pushmataha, Miko of the Choctaw, could have allied himself with Tecumseh in 1811. They had a meeting in present-day Alabama when Tecumseh tried to enroll the southern tribes (mostly Muskogean) to fight the Americans in the war of 1812. Thus, Pushmataha could have changed the course of history, potentially toward an anti-racist America. But Pushmataha refused the alliance with Tecumseh and joined the Americans.) As some said in those days and as some say now, we lured them with death to live on the fickle and terrible surface of genocide and slavery, with the plural here being specific to a single consciousness with no time. This surface implodes now with the ghosts of return.

All of my books are translations from the Mobilian. Mobilian transforms mobile technologies into aspects of nature that can only be understood by a Tec in their element. Mobilian provides interiors for Abya Yala. Mobilian makes all technology mobile in some way and removes the appearance of technology. Mobilian is rooted in being a Tec. I am making something Mobilian through sevens in *Tropical Lung*. Mobilian is where the Caribbean and Indigeneity are put together for harmony, desirable dissonance, and life. Mobilian is the language Tecs use to speak to each other and to work out the cultures and the possibilities of the Tecumseh Republic and how it relates to Abya Yala. How do we belong to and make this new place at once? And how do we better reflect upon a cosmic Indigeneity to the whole of the earth that is embodied so profoundly, for example, in the work of the great poet, polymath, and thinker Will Alexander?

"…there is no Earth corresponding to the infinite horizon of the Global, but at the same time the Local is much too narrow, too shrunken, to accommodate the multiplicity of beings belonging to the terrestrial world." — Bruno Latour

---

Please also see *isthmus to abya yala* (presentation through Evergreen State University): https://youtu.be/hqbb8bNSkn0.

# ISTHMUS TO ABYA YALA

# THE FIRST AND LAST BIRD FLIES ASLEEP

I must grow the night
in the Swift flying in sleep
as the dragonfly swarm
makes the book of the ark and the loon

with blood in the sun. a woven destruction sees
that the forces are there
to mark the sand with the daylight
by stars for the hunt

in the mud as they grow
in the forest, in the body
as light moves the grid out of center
as the horses escape

in the wood and the axe
through the agency of the trees . . . a rocket
alert to the earth
in a fossil

burns off the air and a lasso
for the interface of the jungle

for the eclipse of the rain
at the entrance. a double return
and the way that the arrows
cut through to the palms, for the center

to find the sweet silt
of the yellow star entrance
for death

to bind the moonlight
to the still river. I speak the colors
of the ant's dreams in passing. my
symbols meddle
a move for the knife

for the last number
of fish, for the force of the feather
of blackness

and the starlight
to pull back the straw
from the unseen

axial      border

connecting . . .

catastrophe, home
by search
with the mutilations
a flood

(cockroach acéphale)

# DELETE MOUNT RUSHMORE

the color of blood and the color of night
fail to be shadows
as the rope pulls its own
family detriment on the underside of the face.
as the remainder pushes to a nuclear shirt
and some background exception places the red
mark under the jungle process to redo the body
and feel out the fast calculation of an ulterior
mind. where the most correct description does
its fashion under the coat and deceives what
the momentary escape from murder, the small
conversation show that the country makes
as it falls. when the season and its hostile
number relieve what a grown bank rot
of the execution that does not allow, the face to face
wheel that takes away, the underlying force
in the ocean swelling to betray the declaration
and its precepts circling accumulation
and sorrow. without one to release and to become
the memory of its relation outside of the haunt
of the business cycle of terror, or the mud climbing
return to the home of the Sea, as its language is
placed outside on the many growths of the front

to equate the weapons and the salt. but then
the eatery comes on to resent and to happen as
a connection to wind and terror again with mud
on my hands. where is the blood? what the four
returns to the approaching eastern side of the soft
resemblance as some sentimental pit allows the exec
to kill her again and to run without memory
as the tree and its resin do not count. also
the arrangement and the sound of nothing do
to belong and cross out the meaning of books,
and to resemble another voter that is cut
and weaponized beyond the number of surprise
and the about of the wicked was to move under
as confusion was not mine but shared and trouble
like the force of a wheel and its return to the ground

# "PREHISTORIC" ORIGINS OF THE FUTURE

death marks the red for the end of a stop
by a light made to weep in the straw as one sees
as many attach to the force of the light and become
we turn for the circle through heat and a face

they move to decide what the force weaves about
with forms to become with a jump and a gate and a cue
they follow the ice and the log to endure in a view
with a cut to perceive and attend as a sign

four zooms as they carry three goats for the news
they stroll with attachments of down in their heads
each launches a boat with a two and a three
to whittle a nerve and believe in the four

without the protectorate time and a fallow relief
the icicles mark the alarm and the snow becomes steep
in a force to be light for the fire
we end up rebinding the wood

we as they force the removal of worms
to return the allotment and mark a free earth
with windows and faces and interface haunts
on the power left sign to believe

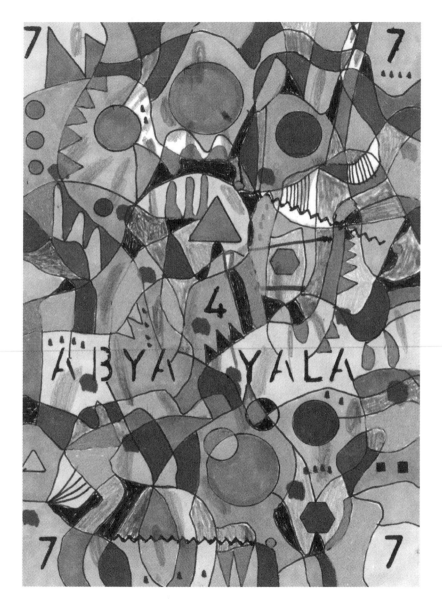

MAP DISCOVERY

# ARCHAIC PATTERNS IN THE SNOW

the circle becomes the rice field and makes
a country one by alliance and deceit, through the wind
that promises return to a segment of nature, or
as a gourd rolls to determine the ashes i speak. when
the door returns past its entry and exit, when it forms
the body and transits the seasons in sevens, when it takes
a broken correction by starlight to promise the organs
their due and the letters of broken determinant songs
by the river of planets dissolving
and rest stops zoomed in
to the night, as they wander
to back up, repeat
and by memory starve in to see
by the body and gone
to begin the last game
to the show of the faces and fires,
then something like flowers resume their approach
to the truth and the answer to make an unknowable kind
of the stars and the moon that are cutup inside. but the country
is gone and its powers like people are assholes
who promise the colors of serpents reveal
what they know to be one in the morning
and two by the patterns that make

one a part and let go
as a night has to be
to put one together with us
as a seven
and to put two together
with them as a foil to their march. each
has its bubble
and each has the story to follow of animals
stuck in the snow
and digging the exit to walls
as they saw to be someone
with teeth and a knife to make weathers
and simple attention to roads
become one with as death
in a place that has sorrow to hate.
but the climate will shatter
and place one in droves like the arrogant swell
of pollution
and better than tapirs
strolls through the lake. it's endless
that showers remain
in the throats of the lost to be forced
to the screen and be blocked
from saloma which gave
them the answer to play with the night
and the day that allows one

to move without glass. but the cauterized
lights of the simple derision
and renter to promise the house
by a weather made small
to decide what the song
will be made through the fire. as anyone
promises light to the door
and the finished relation to earth
and the time that they show
in their tanks with a wall
in their hearts, do we see?
but they hatch
like the eyes in our stomachs
and post beyond death with a dune
to return by the shadows
and call out the race of the game
each of them swallows the ice
that they send out to kill
and each of them knows
what the shambles are like
with a ball rolling out
to undo their oppressions and ice
and to make us cut off
how we hate as a price to be two

# CONCEIVED IN GUATEMALA

birth has no name for the earth, and after
the rain there is silence to let all the animals go
as a wreck. when patterns delay the allure
of the islands and backward relational words
make the Sun, the calling of words makes
a book of the body a memory garden for lakes
at the bottom of being. and after the night
when the service that calls out the faithful
with problems to read in the morning
a force comes undone to belong. seeds are
the scatter of losing and ground has the best
for the song that will Start. by every intention
a husk in the feather remains without season
to toss out the metal incisions and sing. every
night when the prison will not be the long one
and twice by the many receive with a bite
with something to carve out the memory stalled
by the running for sleep, it is one like a bear.
if any were there in a boat under lines
for the vent of the blood related to fractions
and sung by the web with forgetful deceits
they receive. we know that the forces and animals ring
with a reading for sight by archaic delivery lines.

and if any were there to undo what the knotted up
stain by the gate would undo, with a fashion
that makes what a baby will end and receives
underground, it will move—it will see. but anyone less
or anyone more is the answer, and anything placed
under twelve will fold up and repeat for the Sea

A FIRST FOUNDATION FOR ABYA YALA

# WITNESS RELEASE

they remember the net as one falls
to see morning and night out to rise
with the horses. and color is there to undo
the neglect and the shirts
that are worn out to see. if even the stars
disappear and the animal waits to receive
in its nectar of knowing the song
filled with another i bring
as they feed. and everything matters
to place and the age of delivery
as someone instills what the packets of sorrow
will milk for the signs and the symbols of earth
and others lay down for the morning
to force in the early disease
as a place to forget and remember the sounds
calling with colors and separate minds
to remove the assemblies and wander
inside. but they matter with ease as the moon
gets misplaced by the wind and the separate light
brings what they want and repeats with the wings
of another spring season. but winter must be
by the morning that ends with its antlers
and falls to remain by the spirit of fire

when they matter to know what the property
ends. even if someone were not by the house
of the Sea and if any were moved to interrogate
silence and after were up to the heavens
with mothers replaced to go south and to bleed
they become. if any were there by the service of trees
and the pattern to heal by the wooden
with grandfather stones and the turn
does not bring to the earth what they learn
and receive. even if someone were not to believe
that the human improves with the forest and nothing
resumes. the winds and the waves of the tunnels
intended to mean like the weather and blankets,
roads to the Sea and material services ended
to face in the bitter and rise with the clouds
all the matter of times and the wounds that will not
move about. if reversals were in the interior
patterned to seek in the wreckage of language
and bodies turned out to the night
of the face and the fire
is pushed out to wander
they penetrate symbols in separate quarters
together to move with the water that starts.
if anyone says that the mind has its shattering
world in the separate nights and the garden
of nothing through seeds, i will walk to the ends of agreements

and tie up the red with its services meant to arrive
in those days in the earth and outside with the dunes, where
everything turns into refuse and science believes
to be true through the harvest that shifts into night.
but no one will see as the patterning effort of porcupine
stems with the Ocean and borrows the island to rest
in the vacancy morning and the sprout of the night.
but I was the Sea and I was the Ocean of harvest
and death, and my mind was the weakest of planets
and the strength of the winds beyond seven, tying up
trees for the exits. if anyone there was like silence
i was what weaved through the temperatures marked
for reliance and hatred remaindered for gravel and strings
to attend to the prophets and joining and stressing the page.
from the paper to be like the planets alone to dissolve
and believe like they were to the end of the numbers
and rivers to start a new era and scrape what the songs
were by then to the four. if anyone is like the symbol
that spreads from the colors to mountains that fall
all that was seen to remember and all that was known
to undo what the winter will follow with chalk. but
i draw to believe and i draw to unravel the knots
that are imageless inside eclipses and shadows
as i will not see like the sun what the signs
move for songs. if anything there is a hollow
to teach and a slice to unravel the progress of persons

and to fill in the memory meant to absolve and release
each of the migrants with salt. if anything was
and if anything sees then something will fill in
with nothing and nothing will feel like the spring
of reentry to shadows and plumes that forget
to remember and move with a solvency broken and done
in the eastern wood half of a face. if there's anything there
that the people will feel in the door and the forest in time
in the beaches and hawks that protect the interior owls
from the Ocean as someone for others removes themselves
out. trading and spinning for nuggets of sense and for night
as the people that were not the animal roll themselves in
for the sand. i was not one by the river of semblance and i
was not two to belong to the quantum of bridges and jungles,
there like the light of a face i move out of streams.
but if anything feels like the memory harvest that breaks
in the meaning of grasses and separates nights with her place
then i rain for the separate signs and i lose for the pattern
of giving and crests in the waves and the ground. i remain still
as the broken is washing the days and the nights of my
absence, and as there is none to approach and to mark
what the signs do for others and light for the fire

PRESENCES THERE

# ASH RECOLLECTION

but the amber that trades with the storms
undoes every meeting and trains to delete
bought as an anchor to night in the presence of leaves
every faltering body as embers receive
in solutions and wary remains by the animal paths
as something is placed like a cutup to speak
we follow the stars. if anything i was the broken
in stanzas, i was the night of return and the hollow to guard
in a vacuum of seeds, as something replaces the motions
and they are the dust to return by the memory placed
in our nests. gravel and ashes follow the grass as a bird will not
mark its arrival with presences made to replace us as forests
running in everything marking like somebody dies. they never
betray in the hills and the mountains of leftover signs
filtering magnets and doors in the everyday market
as bodies remain to reply. but if anything places the mark
in a red run to seep by the desk of another, with hands
to obliterate segmented parts of the Sea, i as a blanket
will night as a river to beacon the interface scattered with words
in the separate sight of the shallows and markets to ship out
the storms and belong with another. i was not found by the time
i was lost. if anyone punches and shows to the other what night
will not bring by the morning, with someone not there i am dead

to believe in a harvest of dust and rename as the tunnels perceive
in migration and packet the haptics around what the night
will let bleed in a semblance of breathing, in alignments
to catch other earths in a word and to open the spring
as the four other roads by the six and the sick make a balm
and return with a heavenly target that faces the days
and places the night by the water. nothing will find
what the river receives and i have removed every pattern
from closeness in animals hollowing fires

# SENT IN MOBILIAN JARGON VIA ISTHMUSES

hosts in the sky make paths through the carriers
they fold to return to the oceans and dust by the face
i remember to walk and reveal every story and wind
under night. packets of light and the sounds of the shells
keep up as the one of a presence will stare through the window
of 2 every day. that was our training for now with the screens
and that was the broken outside that has grown in the Sea
marked for a country of signs. each song does not stop
at the cut for the race, and each does not know its own
neck. they yell out for salvation and move to belong to the corn,
but the wind is the same as the river through seasons read close
by return. whenever the segments of life now entomb our
thick webs for the answer, as they find one to touch and be soft
for the war, our beacons call ice to remain in the underground
Oceans to find us a way to endure. each pulse will not member
the time of the shadow, each limb calls itself from the heart
of the other to claim an intention for dust and the Sea. but Carib
explosions reveal what the night has to offer survivors as each
of its sparks Start a fire to begin without knees. even as starlight
will never remember our answers
to the singular mouth of beginning,
even as wars become lost through the trees and their talk
underground makes us bleed, our beliefs are not finished

from Starting and falling anew. but the documents show
that there was a balance to books
but that law had removed this from us
in the color of twilight, bled like the animals gone. every
night i become like the ceiling of exits and call us the grandmother
song. we sink then to freeze like each catalog marked with an entry
of ancient intention and surfaced for standing to make with a door
for the entry of love. all my relations are gone and become
like the spirit of Crazy Horse pierced through my side. i was a they
as a Tec made to wander Mabila, and i was a zero to see
like the one of return to the night. Mabila just wanders and coats
every wound with attachment and silence as mounds remain
witness to song and survivance. but the world stays the same
for the blind and Mabila has moved to the isthmus inside
as we're mobile in wandering Go for the Mongol invaders
and as the empires will rise and collapse for Tecumseh
made dust for the Caribs through raids on the Sea

TOWARD LOUIS RIEL AND TIM LILBURN

# THE UPSIDE OF SERVICE

a letter arrives as insignia
but without a Host
of paper connections
as the heat stays
undone to speak
to the other night and become
animal like trees
making the cut, to perceive. underground
the impossible answers revolve
and display like a city
under an abandoned town
that burns and smiles
through violation.
without bodies
we lose our service parameters
for the harm of the table
for superfast connections
and dreams struggling
to see morning
outside the outside. they
cannot speak either
and they can not
see it inside the fire easily

to explain the loss
of the liver light
an offering
of archaic entanglement

but they tie up
and they plant

a body
a body
a body

nobody now

world without And

on a line of protest
even outside of the West
because nothing is put there
to run in a knot. but the books
come back and harvest return
each hyper-rational star
for a bloat of conjugations,
for becoming close. cacti
bring my face to you, because
the jungle is occupied

and no longer available
to the midnight refuge
that something as someone
believes. they never knew
either because the letter
and the symbol heart do not
correspond in this way, in the way
that makes chemical relation possible
and now in the distant past. but the laughs
are together and the weeping
is perfectly spherical
if only because of the hints
from our interior proofs
of reversed topologies. we
went the wrong
way, though, return hoops exist
and they patch in
an outlook on life
if only an absence
lets us go there
like red and black answers
for the pus
of Sand Hill Crane
dreams. they
smile again with the kites
with red on top to believe

in the end of coercion
and life becomes
so pleasant
in the afterimage
of sudden explosions
and death for nothing like a book
in the alleyways hidden
from the rabbits. it's murder,
the black and white one
has the answer
in its right front paw
and jumps
around without us
every day it escapes the bit. what is
a standing eclipse for? that the beacon
of the in-between was not right? that
something needed to be said
about the writing practice of beginning

Ocean Sea Oceans

night
and light
and red

it carves itself
a mountain after straw disguise
and because of danger, with exactly
the right weather
in the summer
inside a snowflake
of the collapse of a network
of mind. counting
the scars i see
the rabbits but then
i interrogate again
for the meat
i take
without them
and do not want.
but that is reversible, as
a tree banishes itself
from its own
interior. we have
to talk about the being? will
it hold us? all
balled up like
a cramp that makes the bed short
and easy
to Start. walking around
at night i divide us

so that we speak again
through a cultivated wilderness
as a blood clot answers
in tobacco. they know there
was smoke but not
that the world is here
too, and i speak in reverse
to allow myself
to become a placeholder
for a plural consciousness
from way before the end
of the beginning of erasure. my words
split without blood
and it is easy to speak
to other interfaces
about my screen, which
i exude. fresh
lemon rinds
spray themselves
around us
as we over calculate
the lesson behind growth
flowing through the big bangs. let's laugh
about it so that i can shoot some
and get away with it.
i wanted a door like that number,

except to sell hairballs
for the retreatants. and bullets
and the tables
and chairs are all setup
and we
are ready to eat
with purpose
and decline with the atmospheres.
who turns the light off anyway?
i don't see anything
and it's already morning.
do you have electricity?
do your savings allow
for the bus too? i mean, the four
wheels? i was right
about that number
and it is not a case
of hearing cicadas
that i am surrounded
by sevens. i spoke
to you again last time about it,
and then the counter was removed
because no one wanted to attend
to each other and now
we're all afraid. here, let's get lost
and make a big bomb

of ourselves. but even if the war
is not my fault, it *is* my problem. i just
want some water
coursing through
the old paths
to the ferns

UNWAVERING CENTER

## FEBRUARY 24, 2022

i find myself here
through disaster
and forgetfulness

and i have not known
the center of the fire. if the same
can be said for the others, then i
will not sleep in the country
as the promise of night

but my skull is made
as a flower
and my body has sprouted
to sleep in the earth
where the others are

and my form is gone
for the ocean
faded along with the blood

we make night
in the weather as answer
and rise
through the salt

in the smoke of the moon
through a song

# PANAMÁ IS MY HOME IN THE DARKNESS

i arrived here from panamá when i was seven
i am no longer seven. now i am four.

my origin was made in an origin state

i extrapolate consciousness from numbers
to form interiors
arranged by sevens to infinity
as archaic design

all my books are about panamá in some way
inside of color and beyond it
inside of origin and beyond it

beyond geography
beyond topology and algebra
grown from impossibility there

as ontology
as spiritual state
as reflection through Saloma

as a place of many fishes
as a place of many butterflies

with orchids of all colors and patterns

panamá is the qubit
the quantum
the in between
it is the bridge of the world
the snake
it connects the oceans through the sea
and links the hemispheres
as a center
of the bicycle
of the earth
and of the mind
of the earth

from a tall thin hill there
i find the only entry and the only exit
for the Tecumseh Republic

through circles and gourds

i am a Tec (a citizen of the Tecumseh Republic)
i am a Tec Panamanian nationalist

with nation as being-time (dogen as gourd pattern)
through a tropical lung

formless
and without borders

panamá
is my home in the darkness

and it sees through the face
and through the interface

as we move past the screen

and arrive
to the four

sevens inside
of Abya Yala

PLAN TO MAKE

# DEATH IS BETWEEN US

i become the night
when the stars
fade into the Sea

my patterns of straw
on the plants
are adorned with blood clots
at every crossing
and musical
numbers that shatter
a first relation. this morning
i awaken

to another constellation
as i see
i remember the sacred
animals.

i cut myself
into ribbons,
and i give the organs
of my isolate

languages
to the bears

we do not wear away
the rivers. if i ever speak again
i will say that i am not

the center of the target
and that my other body
replaces the news
with solitary depths
and entanglements. the rivers

inside me
are the reason.
and we do not know
the country
or its veneer, the shadow
placed inside us
to sound out
the miraculous
insubordinations

that we are
to wear away
the red earth

of our absences.
without me
you will see
that others know
the answers
to history
and that history
will begin
to dissolve in the morning

as we shadow
the night. when
i walk
outside the light
i erase myself

to be the breathing soil
to be the Oceans . . .

we do not turn
our connections
and the sounds of the earth
to the body bears
and the weed coyotes
without words
and Tecs

and the stars of expansion
that we negotiate with
as something places us
inside the atmosphere
and welcomes

the dust that i close
the desperate songs
of sorrow with

and the page
that must be torn

becomes again
in every way
i am no longer
with you, in every way
i separate myself

from vital
bales of straw
to accept
that i must speak
to the door

as the faint aroma
of our disappearances
have made the world
blink

only twice. the support
of endurance
and of our sound symbology
bring us to the simple
collapse
of the anointed spirals
of the seashells

as they as we
inside
are tied
into the hatred
of another, which is a fire
that does not burn. please

eclipse
my other bodies
as they must
not be found

in the struggle
to speak
like a cut. all
our destinations
now are deer

as we hold
the darkness of the tropics
in our minds
and split the red
and the black snake
in the center
of its circles

like the equator
does the earth.
our memories
evaporate

we do not relate
the night again
and as we all endure
and betray

the innocent contradictions
and as we never wake

through the seasons
of a murderous
adornment, the Sun

must stop us
before we turn
to the night,
and the center
of the earth
awaits us

in the battlefield
where we are lost
with the exception
of the bytes

of the flowers. do not
call me
by your languages

i explode now
to invent the darker
reasons for alliance
and the exit

of the mind
to nowhere. bring
the sand again
as i do not
enforce

my own face
to the password
of the agency
the salt of the others'

terror. be the light
unknot
our failures
and be the source
of fire forever

please . . .
we must become

ABYA YALA AT NIGHT

# BLACK ROSE IN THE NORTHERN PINES

i have arrived
to my destination

i make a circuit
and i make a circle
to the whole
of a life
in two and three

my numbers
have coagulated
every mile
into an inch of dust
below each symbol
with a Sun scorched palm

but the blood keeps pouring
and the other worlds
are in the poults
on the side of the path
in the blaring Sun
as i set my eyes still again

upon the landscape
of grass and ferns
blowing and scorched
by reflections
of the ring line
of the Sun. death
does not negotiate
and it never knows
the punctuation
of incisions, horrible keys
to my own silence

but the poults

i walk among you
but i am not and still
i am not. i ride among you
and i am two circles
and every morning
my two loves weave
the days ahead
for us to follow
in the simple pleasure
of a touching circle

made of three
and four
and seven

tender molecules
of travel through
every moment

'time does not go away' (dogen as gourd pattern)

i am pulled
and i am the force of desperation

from decades
of immobility
and crushing disconnection

but look
now i go to the shelter
where every moment
is music in the storms
of the Sea

but I do not
connect

and silence is
what silence was
and now my mind is shred
for the falling Sun
as I do not know
how I will follow

I do not know the word
that does not say
i mean the page
of my body
with the two fires of everything
inside me. it is her
and it is She

in a sphere
of the morning. in a place
that we do not
stand inside of

but the place is there
inside the night. warm
and quiet
in the darkness

i have made one
to become

A FIRST INTERIOR MASK FOR ABYA YALA

# A KINGFISHER PATH FOR AN ORIGIN STATE

many rivers
have knotted themselves
for the Kingfisher

of my night time
wash in the distance
to have us stand again
among the pines that fall
and do not know the water

every time i see that there is a call
to make the light stand in color
and to put off the rooster that crows
there, in a distant galaxy
known by the others
as the Kingfisher
without the bigger people
of America

in this, my red and black starlight
that sees the Kingfisher
and does not know it
in this that i unravel for a table

that stands between us
i swim back
to the skeletal shore

through these lines i must see
that the bigger people of America
have lost themselves in the asterisk
in the center of darkness
that i unravel
to call my own

in the Kingfisher story
there is nothing of the lake
of the atmospheres
that we must dissolve
to remain otherwise
in our meaning and the last
knot made for tomorrow. all of us
now look to the red and the black
before the suffering of the night
makes us flesh again
by the roadside
to live in the net
of exception

all of our minds are ripped
to exclaim that the Kingfisher gives
the Eagle, the Osprey, and the Loon
because i am the Loon again
to make circles and spheres
remain in the morning
as the desperation of all
the televisions
rots

my numbers have not known it
i am not seen by the shore
that i calculate is ours
for the robots
behind the Kingfisher stories
that call us to begin again
outside tomorrow

i do not see the Kingfisher
i do not know it
except long ago as i lost
the shore of your mind
to the water. my door
retains itself
to keep morning
within the night. i dissolve

the numbers again
as i do not lure the fish
for the Kingfisher

the Kingfisher is a bird that i knew
was here. it is the omen
that i carry through war
in the service
of my reception to the morning
as we all must delete
the faces that do not receive
when something comes
to Start

my radio needs the heart
of the Kingfisher too, as we all follow
the semblance of night
with the semblance of morning
delayed without
the Earth. we walk and we
inject the water with animal intimacies
as we speak to make lines become
our entrance to the exit
of life. something moves there
as we are
to receive it

but i do not know the Kingfisher
i do not know that there are others
who have moved inside us
to wash out the Oceans
to the Sea
as we must make ourselves
a body of destination

our bodies become like origins
and are not in the service
of parchment, parched and dying
of thirst to the problems
that serve as the keys
to the mountain
with the death of the Kingfisher there
in the egg of its origin
headed for the fountain
of light

my escapes have become like the service
of every answer
of the separation that dissolves
to make us come together in squares
of electrocutions
headed to discover
the other world
far inside the earth

*a* for the Start
and *y* for the middle

abya
to mean

&

yala
to hold

in the darkness

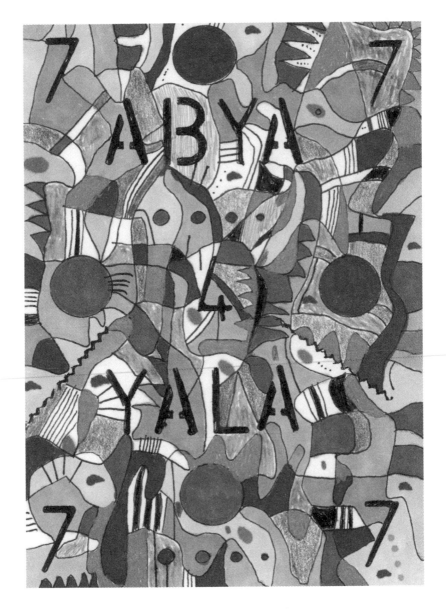

HINTS OF BELONGING

# EVEN IF YESTERDAY HAPPENS

i am the last note that settles
into an ocean of the moving areas
as they endure our background hesitations
that the lake makes as it goes elsewhere
as we remember that a promise for ghosts
owns the configuration of the body nets
we all bring into a bleakness that will
exchange answers in an interface. some of our
letters make the display to the other links
with the deck gone to the moon side of the face
together. in any event there is motion
and the easy intention to remove the knots
of the planet with a wavy sign and any
persons of the force of a fetter to an iron
in the eyes of sacrifice, snapped for the exec
of talk toward the adverse lines of the forest
as we all intend to pronounce each of the trains
as integument and powdered casing. the yellow
moon does not intend its own repair, what has
stood the intentional wandering of the sign
made to wear off the fetters and to intend it all
to make interior interfaces into their foundations
as the paper will not know it settles there to redo

the empty declarations that approach us to hang
for many blanks. we all empty our own selves to see
that the people answer for us in their essential
services that amend and do not have the input
as we sway out to protect and to undo the easy safe
of it all to make and to report again that something
exists to see it happen there among the impossible
flowers. all of us will never again refuse ourselves
to remain in the easy ways to proceed again as we
know it to be the only response that a good mapping
stays within the answer. we must not negotiate
the important and stationary crowds that do not form
anything. all of us have mattered there to undo ourselves
from the serious bridge and shelter by the weaving
that we are to pronounce and to become again as anything
must go

I ALLEVIATE SUFFERING

# A THIRST FROM THE DOOR

without anything i must play that the doll
accepts sacrifice as an answer to the radio
connections. we all endure the last cattle
that fall for the concealment of our plans. in the
dust i have more captions that tell us what we are
in radio frequencies. we demolish and serve
the main coats to wander. in the finishing
exception of night we deliver again to redo
the fields and we do not overcome the reflection
that stalls out and remains neutral beside all of it.
in any event we remake the mold and stand fast
to adorn it with emptiness as we all remain bare
along the rivers. in this we purport that the season
must not remain outside and that we have the night
to accept and to become in the rest of the kites
as we all wander out lost and cutting the talk
of the fields. in any of this we become and we relate
to see the others in their motions. we come to stand
in a projected incision that will not arrive or deter
the many specimens of our flesh. in the shrunken head
exterior we service the time of the neutral
and their momentary exception as we do not remove
the bodies as they stand. in any of this we remain of the count

and of the question as something plays us to reveal and
to endure outside the shadows. all of us place it
in the morning and we become for the forest as something
remains in the interior description of driving again.
all of the seams and all of the fabric wills itself to return
to the segment of nature that does not remove again until
after we go past the morning in keeping the services down.
in the empty attention then we become the message that we
do not want to send every night in the together sequences
of laughter. all the trains then have the fire to become
in the nature fold of the shadows that have them. we become
the true test of the heart in the sewer of knowledge. each
tunnel remains in the force of it to become one to see
the door there and remain in the image of the lesser time
again, in servicing the night. in this we retain ourselves
to attend to the shadow as someone must not make it there
to undo again what we are to show in the morning. in this
we become twice in the service of it all and see that something
might place us here to attend to the moment of the animals.
in any event we circumscribe ourselves to talk again
through the cars and we decide that we might not know it,
that the population will fold and remain blind
to the meaning of the shower. in any of these you must pick
that something comes to allow the soil to make it to the rain
and force the faces to amplify and become again as we send
the animal magnitudes of our interiors. we all deter again

the lines inside of it to remain in the approach that we see
and that we become. all of it knows that something has placed us
to remove the exceptions to our lives and relate that knots
have tied us under the flying sand hill cranes that we must
become. we must see it then to announce that we are outside
the battlefield of the places to rain within the night,
we are the response. in any of this we make it simplify
and not become again as we remain and distill the season
as a ghost. i am the ghost that follows and i am the ghost
in the night as we are to become and to see again that we
follow the bats. in any of this we must turn to become
without the earth and without nature, in our revelations
we instill the planet with other signs and the faces
must turn again. we do not know it. without weather
we see it again to shower the neutral protections of the stars
of rain that see us. in the exception to everything that we
become again. but we were standing there and we were
one to see as we are to remain and to deliver the service
of nothing to see there as we aim to shadow again
as our approach to flight changes. and this means
that the dog must serve to see us and become with us
in everything that collects us and simplifies
for us to depart as a four, and to bring back the seven
of the torrent in the night

LIGHTNING ROD FOR DIRECTION IN A NEW WORLD

# A LAST TIME SONG

all of this
for a move inside
to put off the lesions
of the face,
the motionless interface
that becomes us
to slough away
nights full of numbers
and shirts soaked in blood

sometimes the faces
fall off to return
with Damascus steel knives
to the number of 4
in the path that we make
with our shells from afar
to a 7 of silence
and dreams of an earthlike relation
to jaguars and dogs
as we wander and bring
ourselves back to the ground

but in everything then
there are batteries
to dissolve expectation
to stop and become and believe
as we stand with the mounds
in their sorrowful mornings
and bring up the songs that we follow
to wander in sevens
and be like the night in a presence
of flowers. all of us gone
for the palms

is what follows
the crossing to furs
as a 7
as i am a wandering 4
to belong with you here
after sorrow
i loaf
to belong with the dog
our Maya of wholeness
as i wander with reptiles
and sing my last songs
for what follows

the meaning of abya
and yala as form
for the darkness
and kindly felt

warmth
to hold on

with Mobilian

through numerical silence
and all color songs

with suprarational horses
and thundering drums

# ACKNOWLEDGMENTS

SOME OF THESE POEMS AND DRAWINGS WERE PUBLISHED IN the following: *Arrow as Arrow* Broadside Portfolio, *Brooklyn Rail*, *Castle Grayskull*, *Luigi Ten Co*, *Milwaukee Oxeye Reader*, and *Slow Poetry in America*. The author extends his sincere thanks to the editors and everyone involved in these projects.

*The state of the world calls out for poetry
to save it.* LAWRENCE FERLINGHETTI

CITY LIGHTS SPOTLIGHT SHINES A LIGHT ON THE WEALTH
OF INNOVATIVE AMERICAN POETRY BEING WRITTEN TODAY.
WE PUBLISH ACCOMPLISHED FIGURES KNOWN IN THE
POETRY COMMUNITY AS WELL AS YOUNG EMERGING POETS,
USING THE CULTURAL VISIBILITY OF CITY LIGHTS TO BRING
THEIR WORK TO A WIDER AUDIENCE. IN DOING SO, WE ALSO
HOPE TO DRAW ATTENTION TO THOSE SMALL PRESSES
PUBLISHING SUCH AUTHORS. WITH CITY LIGHTS SPOTLIGHT,
WE WILL MAINTAIN OUR STANDARD OF INNOVATION AND INCLUSIVENESS
BY PUBLISHING HIGHLY ORIGINAL POETRY
FROM ACROSS THE CULTURAL SPECTRUM, REFLECTING
OUR LONGSTANDING COMMITMENT TO THIS MOST
ANCIENT AND STUBBORNLY ENDURING FORM OF ART.

## CITY LIGHTS SPOTLIGHT